Caught In a Wave

Caught In a Wave

Poetry of a Hectic Life

DOMINIQUE E. ZSEDENNY

authorHOUSE®

AuthorHouse™
1663 Liberty Drive
Bloomington, IN 47403
www.authorhouse.com
Phone: 1-800-839-8640

Published by AuthorHouse   12/14/2012

ISBN: 978-1-4772-9926-5 (sc)
ISBN: 978-1-4772-9925-8 (e)

Library of Congress Control Number: 2012923722

Contents

· ·

Part I: **My Angel**

Part II: **Relationships**

Intrigue

Turmoil

Family

Part III: Moments and People

This book is dedicated to my family.

No matter what life throws our way, we stick together and stand by one another. Life has been tough on us all, and our love for each other keeps us going strong. Above all, the love I feel for my little boy is what keeps me going day by day.

I would also like to say thank you to the amazing man who re-entered my life after a very long absence; you truly hold my heart, as you have since I gave it to you all those years ago, I am glad I can say I once again feel whole.

Part I:

My Angel

Life Inside

Life,

Growing inside

Bringing a smile

To my face.

Sweet and innocent

Getting stronger each day

Soon to arrive.

Days go by

And the anticipation grows,

Loving this life

Growing inside.

Time to Arrive

The wonder of the world

Each day an event to remember

While the pain, you only hope to forget.

Every joy comes measured by pain,

So this is truly the greatest joy of all.

I love you dearly, above all else,

With you my heart is over flowing

With you in my arms, I find bliss.

Seeing You

So sweet and pure

I thought for sure

You'd have an Angel's golden hair,

With baby blue eyes to match.

You'd be a catch

And all the world would stop and stare.

But you my Angel,

Came to be

With the sweetest look of all.

Chocolate eyes and chocolate hair,

With the brilliance of love in your stare.

Warmth

My bundle

Wrapped tight

Held to my chest,

Is there anything more precious?

My Angel

Bundled from the cold

And held in my arms.

A Gift to a Mom

My Angel is a gift to me

A present in my care.

So that I may love and care

Until my days are done.

I was a mother, the day I knew,

His life was entwined with mine.

And I became a mom in the second

His gaze locked in on mine.

And from that time on, I'll be his mom

Until the end of time and more.

My Angel

Wrapped in my arms

He was perfect;

All cute smiles

And gurgling coos,

I fell in love.

With a yawn

And a stretch of his little arms,

He stole my heart.

My Angel,

My love,

This baby in my arms

This Angel in my life,

Is pure happiness and joy.

Halfway There

I glance at his face,

Over his first bite of food,

And smile in pride at my big boy.

Half a year has passed

Since he entered my world,

And he's halfway to

The first party of his birth.

My precious boy,

With a smile and a laugh,

He goes for bite two;

So happy he is,

This baby of mine.

I love my Angel,

He lights my day

And I smile as he does,

With pure joy

And the love of life.

Elevation

To stand

Such a simple task

For you and I, it is easy.

But in the beginning

It is sure a struggle.

Holding on for dear life,

Pulling up,

Legs trembling

He looks around.

Pure amazement and wonder

Cover his face,

As my Angel stands.

To see the world from this angle,

A new perspective of life,

He smiles, giggles,

And claps his little hands.

With no grasping hands holding him steady

He tumbles to the floor,

Deterred for merely a moment

Before he gets up and tries once more.

Bubble Bath

Blowing bubbles

My baby mine

Splashing wildly

Ducks in a line

Hide and seek

Water ring toss

He plays in the bath

Smiling so joyous

Laughing and splashing

My baby mine

In a bubble bath

My Angel divine

Rescue

Left in that place

I saw him miserable,

I took him out

In a haze of red.

My Angel, he is a sweet thing,

Not the type to leave at all,

Let alone in such a place,

With those awful people.

I marched in and took him

Out of that place,

Away from those people,

Outraged by the condition of that house.

Grime and filth coated that place,

Not fit for a human being,

Let alone an Angel;

My Angel who just turned one.

I refrained from yelling at

And from hitting,

Those incompetent people,

And the sty they inhabited.

The mess was theirs,

But my Angel was not.

It was his dad,

That left him so.

His very own dad,

Who was to watch him that evening;

Left my Angel in that place,

And drove off into the night.

I showed up to see

My baby screaming,

And other kids crying,

While no one tended to their needs.

Many in diapers,

All were dirty,

And tummies were growling

Ever so fiercely.

The state of matters did not stop there,

The dishes were molding from weeks gone by,

And laundry was heaped everywhere,

At least waist high.

He left my baby there,

Without a thought to him,

I stepped in and saw,

And rescued him out of there.

Torn

Away from me,

Out of my arms

He was taken.

With anger and sadness,

I was torn.

My heart shredded

My mind tumbling in darkness,

And my body numb.

When he was taken,

So was a part of me,

A part only he can return,

To my ever aching heart.

Gone

. . . .

Today they took

My Angel away,

Out of my arms

And there he must stay.

They say he is better

In a stranger's arms,

Away from me.

They cannot know

The heart of me,

And how it breaks

Over this day.

They cannot know

The mind of him,

And what he thinks

Of these strangers he is with.

These tears that fall

Are only half for me,

The rest are for my Angel.

Living Nightmare

This torture I endure

This nightmare I live

Isn't going away.

It pains my heart

And tears at my mind,

The role I played in it all.

My Angel and I

Inseparable we were,

Wrapped in love,

And happy each day.

His dad came home

And wanted some time;

I had some problems,

So I agreed, in time.

How could I have known

It would lead us to this?

How could I know

That in the end,

It would have been,

My Angel that hurt the most?

I did not know,

So I agreed

And his dad took him,

For months on end.

I missed him so much,

And called in daily.

But simply it is,

That it wasn't enough.

But his dad messed up

And now they're both gone;

One to the hospital,

For his mental health,

And my Angel was taken by the state.

I try to explain,

To express my side.

But because his dad is gone,

I am held at fault.

I do agree

That some fault lies with me,

For letting my Angel go.

Even though it was to his dad,

I should not have left him be.

But his dad is also a part at fault,

For when my Angel was with me,

He was healthy

And as happy as can be.

But no body sees that.

They see me,

Sitting there on my own,

Feeling lonely and small.

People around me

Stare me down.

Each thinking

The worst of me they can.

They put me on the spot,

Call me a horrible mother,

And say that I neglected my Angel.

I sit there in disbelief

Wondering if this is my life,

This nightmare that won't end.

Needing air,

I feel faint,

The room around me closes in.

This nightmare goes on,

With no concern for me.

They do not see

That I am only human,

Just as they are?

I made a mistake,

I acknowledge and accept that,

But not the mistake

They think I made.

Not the mistake

That I am being accused of,

Not the mistake

For which I am now being held on trial.

My mistake was in trusting,

In relying,

And in having false confidence in,

A single person.

He may have been his dad,

But he is human too.

And it is for trusting him too completely,

That I lay blame at my own feet.

With him my Angel did not prosper,

He lost weight,

Stopped growing,

And no longer did the fun things,

He once enjoyed so well.

I worry about them both now,

But I worry about my Angel more.

His dad is an adult,

He can care for himself.

But my Angel is only a baby,

A little over a year old,

A bundle of pure joy.

He is the true victim here.

But I remain alone,

With thoughts

Circling around in my head,

And a Judge,

Making me feel two inches tall.

The people who claimed

To be on my side,

Who claimed they were

Only here to help,

Now stand against me,

And accuse me of the worst.

Of starving my Angel,

Nearly till death,

And they point their fingers

At the only one here: me.

It is his dad, who ought to be here,

Hearing these charges,

These accusations,

So that he can know what has happened,

So that he can understand,

The ramifications and consequences

For his actions.

But he wasn't strong enough,

He broke down,

And was taken away,

Away from the mess,

Away from the trouble.

So here I stand,

Having to take the blame.

All I want,

Is this mess to be over,

To have my baby,

My little Angel,

To hold him in my arms,

For this nightmare to end.

Raining on Trial

Light, peace, and cleansing

It falls all around me.

Yet it does nothing

To calm this feeling.

This wrenching in my heart,

And the tightening in my muscles.

The rain cleanses the world,

And filters the air around me;

But the turmoil in my life

Is not so easily wiped away.

Missing Angel

Cute thighs

And chubby cheeks,

His laugh carries to me

Over any distance

Near or far.

But now my Angel

Is oh so far,

And I ache to hear

His familiar laugh

From his favorite place;

Curled up safe in my arms.

I need his presence in my life

The joy of caring for my Angel,

Is a treasure I long for, in my life.

A Piece Missing

A piece of me is lost

Looking for direction.

Where does the part of me,

Who is a caring mother,

Go to when there is no one,

In need of my affection?

I cannot turn it off,

This need to care and nurture,

This desire to love and pamper

Some one so small and dear.

So when my baby is away,

What do I do to help this loss?

It is hard to be a mom,

Without a child to give my love.

Each day that passes, I feel the loss,

And wonder if it heals.

Each day I hope this ache in me

Will slowly fade and leave,

But with every day that passes,

The ache just serves to remind me

Of my missing piece.

A Few Tears to Shed

. . . .

Tears of loss and pain

Flow unstopped by me.

I've held in for so long

But now these feelings poor

One drop at a time,

To the newly tiled floor.

So much love and emotion,

Caring and devotion,

I have inside to give.

It sits dormant, no where to go,

As I am a mother without a child.

I have so many hopes,

And dreams that never end,

That someday soon

My son will be home;

With his familiar smile

And the sound of his running feet

Reassuring this fragile heart,

That all has not been in vain.

Missing Changes

So grown you are,

So handsome and sweet,

You capture my heart

With each step of your feet.

I saw the first ones,

Followed by many more

But the next time I see you,

You'll be running through that door.

I was there, to give you a start,

So that you'll be strong

During these times apart.

I, too, must be strong for you,

To bring you home

To the arms that miss you.

And my heart

Longs for that day

We can be together again,

And stay that way.

Each of us have grown,

Becoming more of who we are

And will continue to grow

Into who we will become.

Until that day, you carry with you

The piece of my heart

That will always be yours.

I love you, my Angel

On the Line

At night before bed

The phone is a comfort,

I call my baby,

To hear his jumbled language develop day by day.

Hearing him, and him hearing me,

Gives me the hope

That he will know me still after these months go by.

To the sound of my voice,

He calls, "Ma ma!" out loud,

Bringing a rush of joy

And tears to my eyes.

He knows my voice,

But will he know me?

So much time has elapsed,

Since they took him from me,

And with the line of parents he has passed through,

I fear my memory has become faded

In his sweet little mind.

But through the phone,

And over the line,

I let my hope rise,

That my Angel will still know his mom,

That I am still a big part

Of his very precious life.

Home

Happiness for everyone,

A joy felt deep.

An Angel brought home,

A difficult feat.

A constant battle

A war of wills.

The war was worth it

To bring this thrill.

A baby no more,

A toddler instead,

Everything changes,

His food and his bed.

A room once empty

Now full of life,

His laughter and joy

Back in my life.

When he was gone,

I was bereft,

My heart was empty

Only a shell left.

Now he is home,

My true love and dear,

Him being taken again,

Is my only fear.

Follow the Moon

· ·

Lost without direction

A cold and lonely night

The clouds part to reveal a light,

I'll follow the moon to my heart.

Re living My Nightmare

Reliving my nightmare

Time and again

This roller coaster of emotion

Seems to have no end.

My baby and me

What a perfect team,

Yet all people do

Is try to break us up at all costs.

This time there is no guilt,

This time there is certainty.

I did all that was asked

And still it went bad.

A specialist said there was a problem

Causing my baby not to gain weight,

So my Angel was put on a special diet

That helped him gain, and keep it on.

But there is a pediatrician

Who believes there is nothing wrong

She thinks I starve my little baby,

And so he loses weight.

She tells the State she spoke with the specialist

So now they listen to her every word.

She changes his diet, and his daily calorie intake

Only telling me, "let's see what happens if . . ."

But she lied, of course,

Never did she speak to the specialist, ever,

And now the specialist is mad,

And the state finally caught her in the lies,

Yet they do nothing.

My baby loses weight, and I begin to worry again

We've been here before.

An appointment is made, by worried parents,

And he is weighed, two pounds lighter

Than just a few weeks ago.

I am a worried mom, taking my baby to a doctor,

In search of answers, not accusations.

What I get is a nightmare, the same as before.

The State is called and my Angel is hospitalized.

Days of not knowing pass, with no tests run,

And they take me to court, taking my baby.

Not again. It can't be, but yes. Again.

And I am escorted out of the hospital,

Away from my love, and my life.

I am left empty and alone once more.

Numb Silence

With my heart ripped out

Beating loudly outside my chest

My limbs go numb.

Waves crash in my ears

Then there is only silence

As full numbness sets in.

My mind and body

Are protecting themselves,

And logically I know this is shock

But as the pain is blocked

I don't seem to mind it all that much.

Life would be quiet to live in this shell,

But can you call it living

If your heart no longer beats.

Silent Sadness

In her mind she cries

Tears, each another shadow in her life.

So calm she sits

Her face blank, her body finally relaxed,

The shadows gather in her mind

And envelop her in mist.

Time

So easy to take for granted

The flow and passing of time.

The amount given

To those we love,

Stands out above all.

It is the most precious gift,

The most important of all.

Things come and go,

But time,

Your time,

Is all too finite.

Times of Change

Nothing lasts forever,

Even the deepest sorrows

Must fade

With the passing and flow of time.

An hour, a week,

A mere moment in time,

And all can change.

A mere moment in life

A grain of sand

In the hour glass of the universe.

Yet how detrimental

Each thought and action feels

Each moment that lingers

Before passing into the next.

Emotions

Wild and untamed

Taking over the mind

And controlling the body

Emotions run free,

Wreaking havoc on all

Both near and far.

I Think of You and Smile

Away from you

Life crashing around

I close my eyes

And see your face

It calms me

And I smile

As thoughts of you

Bring me to life

Losing My Way

This path I am on

Feels right but looks wrong

I sense true happiness

Is within my grasp again

Each moment life is changing

I feel a sense of uncertainty

Like nothing currently around me

Is ever going to stay

When I feel this way

I think of your heart

Of your precious smile

And what I can do for you

To bring you home

Into my arms

You are my Angel

My life and my joy

Bringing you home

Is my anchor for now

So I think of you

And no longer do I feel

Like I am losing my way,

But that I have a new start.

Spring Love and Loss

Heart break and loss

Feelings all too familiar

As I say goodbye yet again.

Time lingering

Sitting in the silence

Of the early spring breeze.

I miss him,

With the whole of my heart,

And an hour or so

Is not enough

Before goodbye

Is forced each time,

Never wanting our time to end.

Free yet Chained

Free yet chained,

I want to run.

Away from the dark

Embrace the sun.

So lost in this life

I want more.

Wanting what won't help

It tempts me

But I know better.

Having what I think I need,

I try to be content.

Life is so confusing,

Lost in the tide

Of what is

And what will be.

I may need rescued

From my own disaster

And sooner than I think.

But for now I keep digging

This hole I find myself in.

When I ought to put the shovel down

And climb out,

Instead I dig more,

And jump deeper in.

Can some one help me,

And bring me to light?

I await the days ahead of me

When I can look up with a smile

And say to myself,

The worst is behind me,

Now I look to the sun.

Until that day,

I do not know what I do.

What each day may bring,

And the mess yet to unfold.

Thief

You stole my son, my baby, my Angel . . .

Took him from my arms

And forced me away.

You stole my heart from my chest

For my Angel holds it,

And he always will.

Now you steal my time, the brief time . . .

That I am allowed to hold

And see my baby.

My Wish

Written in fire,

Frozen in ice,

Written with hope,

Frozen in time.

My wish is simple . . .

Plainly written

And boldly stated:

I want my Angel home.

Our Pain and Loss

Once a week was what was deemed

Was enough for me.

But they were wrong, so wrong.

My heart broke in each lonely moment.

Now I do not get even that,

All is cancelled

Lost

Pain and longing

I yearn for his presence

Without it I am incomplete

Lost and wandering.

But I get no consideration,

Instead they threaten

And forbid

My love keeps me strong

As I fall apart inside.

The hurt and pain, too much to bear

Cascade upon me all at once.

I talk to them, try to reason,

But I am shut down

Wounded

They know the hurt they cause

To me, and to him

And it is his pain

That intensifies my own

Beyond my own belief

And his

Torn

His health is on the line

And both our hearts

Two lives torn apart

By ignorance and deceit.

Now they evade everything

My every question

Ignored

I need to rescue him

From this crooked system

But I am at a loss

Of where to go from here

The fight is unending

A constant strain

Weary

But no matter the obstacles

I will over come

Bringing him home,

Is my one desire.

To see it fulfilled

A dream come true,

Imagine

An Hour in Arms

. . . .

Nothing is more soothing, to a wounded heart

Than a hug, and love.

Creating peace, from a heart that has been such a mess

A moment only you can bring me,

A moment of my very own bliss.

Heaven, Utopia, and all other perfect worlds

Dull in comparison

To that one hour you kept me close to your heart.

Wrapped in your arms

Mommy's little Angel

I have missed you so much

And nothing compares

To the feel of your touch.

Heaven, utopia, and all other perfect worlds

Dull in comparison

To that one hour you kept me close to your heart.

Forever mine, my darling mine,

My love forever, for all of time.

Crash

Loss and anger
Bottled up inside
Until they overflow
A public scene

Pain so deep
Within my heart
Flow as tears
Over my face

Legs can't move
The room spins
And I fall
To my knees

Surrounded by loss
The pain cuts
So deep down
I continuously cry

Déjà vu

. . . .

I know I just saw this

It has happened before, I'm sure.

But it couldn't have, really,

The people just got here

And the day has just begun.

But the conversations ring familiar

And the actions can be predicted

In the back of my mind.

Uncertain

The day passes

Same as the last

Only moments marking

One from the next.

I hear your words,

Taken out of context

They go through my mind

And you should see

The shadows they cast.

I feel alone

As the lies are told

And the support I had

Has long since gone

To live a life of their own.

Lost and bewildered

I face the uncertain

Not knowing the moment

When all that is left

Will shatter and fall.

Trying Lies

Life laid out before me

On trial for a life.

Not mine, I fear

But my son's future

Is on the line.

The lies I hear

Hurt my heart

With every beat,

And burn my ears

The anger I hide

Boils on high.

I want to stand

And scream the truth

To all of the room,

And silence forever

The woman telling lies.

She does not care

For the life she holds

And the lives she ruins

With each word.

My stress is escalated,

My worry is high,

And my hopes are being dashed.

Hours have passed

No positives are shown,

And as the lawyers return

We are told to wait.

Postponed again

Another day spent

With life on hold

Not knowing if tomorrow

Will change the lives

Of those around us,

But above all the life

Of a two year old Angel

Whose life is truly on the line

Hanging in the balance

On this day;

A day that now, has to wait.

Panic and Fear

Panic and fear

Gripped in a vise

Around my heart and mind.

No courage lingers

Away it ran

And I am at a loss to find

Strength to move past

The fear of my nightmares

Suddenly coming true.

Like the first time

They want to judge

To manipulate and blame.

They've built their case

On lies and deceit

In their attempt to frame

A mom, that's me,

Of the very worst crime

There is in all the world.

In this moment

I seek to find

In my mind, some serenity;

And in that courtroom

I hope there is

More truth than lies, and some clarity.

But the deck is stacked

And the cards are dealt

And I've been left with the losing hand.

Ten days to go

And no lawyer around

Is able to handle this case.

I've been there before

Without lawyer or friend

Forced to stand alone in that place;

The nightmares are real

And they plague me still

When I think back on that terrible day.

So I sit and I ponder,

Thinking of ways

To prepare my heart for the pain.

But no matter how

I may think I'm ready,

The day will still drive me insane.

So I try to sleep

And wake each day

Knowing each day brings me closer to my nightmare.

Back at Square One

. . . .

Forgotten is the progress I had made before

Forgotten is the work that has been put in this case

Instead I deal with the realization

That nothing I do will ever be good enough for them.

I have been placed on this carousel,

And it continues to spin,

Throwing my life in shambles around it,

As I struggle to keep up.

What they ask of me is to ignore the injustices,

To ignore the pain caused each moment by them,

Instead I am to jump through their hoops

As one by one they ignite.

It is crazy to do the same thing

Time and time again,

Each time hoping for a different outcome

Than the one that came before.

I have been placed on this carousel,

And it continues to spin,

Throwing my life in shambles around it,

As I struggle to keep up.

A Burden Lifted

Luck breezed into my life today

So long since his last visit

My life had been lacking

Missing even the smallest trace of it.

With his presence he brought

The defense I was lacking

And on top of that,

The best in the area.

With his presence came the calm

The storm may be coming still

But my world is in need of a pause

And the troubles to be still.

It may not be over, but it's on it's way.

Now I need to care for me

As the feelings kept inside are released

Tumbling out of control.

With the chaos comes the tears

The nervous heart beats and the fears.

The need for calm is utmost now

In all aspects of my personal life.

Death of Privacy

The start of these social sites,

The allure at first,

Draws us all in.

But with each person entrapped

The whole world is involved in

The death of privacy.

It was a slow death,

Creeping up through time

Until finally each person

Held part of the blame

For the death of a right

That was once so revered

The death of privacy.

So when a life falls apart,

It is entertainment to all,

And the trauma of few

Is exploited by many,

All due to

The death of privacy.

Privacy was not

The sole victim of attack,

The truth as well,

Took a brutal blow.

The chains of gossip

Fabricated lies,

Passed on and on

Through the space of time.

No body cares though

That truth has now been slaughtered.

Two tragedies,

Affecting us all,

But the deaths are never mourned

Because everyone is too busy to notice.

Scandalous Words

Random people posting comments
None really knowing the truth of the matter.
Hurtful remarks and straight out lies
Fill pages and pages, and what can I say?
It is not fair, having to read the bitter remarks,
Written about me, from people who do not know me.
Some are good, some are terrible; none of those, do I appreciate,
As reading them hurt.
Chains of gossip, nothing more;
People who feel they cannot do something,
Instead trying to write about it.
I thank those in my defense,
Those who care, for my son and I.
And to those who speak negative,
Without truth to back up their claims,
I say to you all:
Live your life, and let me live mine,
Keep your poisonous words to yourself,
And do something positive in this world.
Writing all of these scandalous words,
Does no one any good.

Three

This day marks joy

A celebration of birth;

A day of thanks

For everyday that has come before,

But it is marred.

The joy turns to sorrow

As I think of those days;

The past of pain and turmoil

I've been put through for so long.

You are three now, my Angel,

And still you hold my heart;

But each day cruel people

Find ways to break it apart.

I have gotten stronger,

Yet I've become such a fragile thing,

And in every breath I take

I miss you more and more.

Your smile and your laughter

I only get for moments,

Outside my night time dreams.

So many things have been taken from me,

Like the milestones in your life,

That I can't ever get back.

Steps of independence,

Toilet training and reading;

Helping you with nightmares,

And your words that just keep growing.

I have been forced all this time,

to the out skirts of your life . . .

but even still, my love for you stays strong.

My Angel, my boy,

There is so much I wish to say:

I love you, I miss you,

And I want you home so much!

But these things get stuck

Along with the lump

That is perpetually in my throat.

The day of your birth

Is always a joy to me,

And I wish that someday

The world will stop taking that joy from me.

Seeing Her

So much, I've been through:

Turmoil, at her hands,

Heart ache, from her words.

Much time, has been spent to

Avoid, all contact with her.

The thoughts, that come to mind

Include, the many bad memories

Starring, her and her cruelty

At me, it has been directed

Wrongly, but she refuses

To see, the error in her

Judgment; the opinion she formed

Too soon, without supporting proof.

The sight, of her face, other times,

Before, has crushed my hopes,

Tightens, my heart in my chest, as

Outrage, boils through me at

Her role, in this twisted play.

The harsh, judging look in

Her eyes, cast down upon me,

Still the, breath in my lungs

And the, pulse at my wrist;

My mind, however is busy as ever,

The thoughts, provoked by her and the

Many, pictures in my mind could

Worry, even the sanest mind.

Her role, though unavoidable

Could have, been played with more grace

Than she, has ever cared to show.

Each day, I remind myself that

Her role, is a temporary one,

And I, will not be tortured

By her, forever.

The pain, though unbearable now,

One day, will be a thing of

The past; like the whole of this

Story, concluded but

Still told, in the days to come.

By then, the pain brought on by

The sight, of her sneering face,

Will be, a memory,

Like the, so many things

She has, done and said

To hurt, me and the ones

I love, in this world;

My son, the most.

Low

The nerve of her,

So underhanded,

She stoops to spying

While I am trying

To remain far away

From her menacing presence.

She disgusts me

With her crooked ways,

Spying on me

While I work today.

I stay clear of her

Throughout my day

But several times I have felt

Her eyes seek me out.

In crowded common areas

I understand the inevitable,

But to track me down

To the room I'm working in,

A class room of students

All there to see and hear,

The guarded glances,

And whispered comments

As she underhandedly

Coerces my coworkers

To dislike me as she does.

So low she is stooping

To spread a bad word,

Held with no truth,

But still she persists.

I marvel at her nerve

And I dislike her actions

As she tries to alienate

Me from all others.

So wrong and crooked,

So low and distasteful,

But I guess that is just her.

Silently I still try

To stay far away from

Her menacing glares,

And the poison in her every word.

Sorrow at Good News

Emotions reeling,

The sadness is strong;

Though why,

I still struggle to know.

Another day in court,

And the ending news was great,

My freedom is being granted

Albeit slowly in steps.

I recognize the excitement,

The happiness of this step,

The importance of this moment,

Yet I still fight back the tears.

Sorrow surrounds me

In every waking moment,

Decreasing interest and appetite

Causing me to lose sleep.

I find no logic

In the sadness I feel,

The news was good,

But the trauma has been real.

Years of abuse

Emotionally and mentally

Have piled up together

Drowning my good moment.

The years that have passed,

I can never get back,

The moments I've missed

Can't ever be rewound.

I feel robbed of my life,

But now they offer a small piece of it back.

A piece that should never have been taken,

Had all truly done their part.

The sadness brought on by the loss,

Never seems to fade

And to the people who should be responsible

There is a price that has yet to be paid.

A Visit

. . . .

At work today,

She dropped on by

Quite unexpectedly.

I expected the worst

From times before,

But I was in for a surprise.

The scathing look

And upsetting words,

Never came.

Instead my knees

Were taken from me,

And my jaw lay helpless

On the classroom floor.

Her smile disarmed me,

And further did her words:

An apology of sorts

And an offer of friendship;

Peaceful living

And cooperation in the changes

That were coming on strong.

The class just stared

In quiet surprise

As their assistant principal

Spoke for some time,

Before delivering

A quick hug

To their unsuspecting substitute.

My knees did not return

Until an hour later in the day,

though my jaw recovered itself

Enough to issue the next set of instructions

To a class that surely was

As bewildered as I.

Floored

News, the news hit me today,

Home, my baby was coming home,

Joy, I felt the joy and wanted to scream it out,

Piece, a piece of my life returned

A piece of my heart I thought forever gone,

Fell back into place with a thud,

And a quick smile came to my face.

Shock, my mind faltered at the initial shock,

Her, hearing the news directly from her,

Friend, a woman once an enemy, now thought of as a friend,

Thoughts, the thoughts have swirled in my head all day.

My Angel, once I thought he was forever gone,

But I fought on, each moment hoping and dreaming

Of the day I would hear this news.

Brave, I've had to be brave,

Wait, so long I've had to wait,

Games, oh the games they played,

Pain, each moment they brought me pain.

A piece of my heart I thought forever gone,

Fell back into place with a thud,

And a quick smile came to my face.

The priceless news,

My baby's coming home,

Shook my heart back into place.

A month she said,

So long to wait for a desire so strong,

Yet so short to wait considering the long time apart.

But still each day,

It wears on me,

Hurting my heart,

Pulling my emotions,

And scarring me.

News, the news hit me today,

Home, my baby was coming home,

Joy, I felt the joy and wanted to scream it out,

Piece, a piece of my life returned

A piece of my heart I thought forever gone,

Fell back into place with a thud,

And a quick smile came to my face.

Betrayal

Plans were made, and I told them to you,

With hopes of them coming true.

Instead you altered every one, with plans of your own.

My little boy, my only son,

I wanted this time with him.

You say you understand,

You know the time we've been forced to spend apart.

But despite all that,

You betray my trust,

And dash my hopes to the ground.

You take my plans and make them your own,

And take my son from my sight.

How could you think this was okay with me?

When you know the pain I must feel.

I tell you each time

I spend time in your presence

The pain the separation causes.

But you ignore all that,

And take my son, as I am forced to sit silently.

If I argue,

Or put up a fight,

It can only back fire on me.

I tried still, to use logic and court,

To persuade you let us be,

But you ignored my pleas,

Still betrayed me,

And caused this hurt inside of me.

Cruel Devil

A moment of shock

All turns black and white

As the pain sets in.

Betrayal cuts deep

Unseen blood begins to pool

As my broken heart bleeds.

Lies and truth are jumbled here

Each lost to the other,

Her voice loudest of all.

Indeed her worst

Yet not nearly her first

Betrayal to one she called friend.

Pain, tears, and blood fill the box

They call a room;

All eyes on her, all else unseen.

Her villainy has earned her a name

Never spoken in her presence

Depicting the cruelty in her nature

And the true devil in her heart and soul.

Stab Wound

The knife in my back

Was aimed at my heart

And thrown by a witch.

She pretended friendship

Long enough to betray

Before showing her true identity.

Hugs and smiles were her approach

Declarations of peace and friendship in place;

Her venomous fangs secretly tucked away

As she conned her way into my life.

Words of kindness to my face

Do nothing to sooth the piercing pain

Coursing through my being

Radiating from that knife.

Her religious beliefs

Did nothing to prevent

The crucification at her hands

In that courtroom today.

Cry Me a River

Over and widely used

This expression of sorrow,

A river of tears.

It's my turn now,

As the tears emerge

And flow into

A river of my own.

The Blue Shoes

. . . .

Upon first sight, I thought how nice

They got him a new pair of shoes.

My thoughts had been pure, until I learned,

Until I put together all the other clues.

Now the sight of them, make me cringe.

Knowing how high the price was to pay;

I hate knowing what he had to do for her.

If he was old enough to understand, what would he say?

She coached him to act and say

All the things she wished

All the while bribing my boy;

My dreams she was trying to squish.

A bike, a motorcycle, and those blasted blue shoes

Was the prize placed over his head

A prize he won at the price of innocence

All for the things he said.

To achieve her plan she used my son,

Keeping him from me, day after day.

All the while bribing and coaching him

Each day on the things he had to do and say.

I hate the prizes she used in her fight:

The bike and motorcycle are beyond my sight

So it is merely the thought of them that I truly dislike.

But those terrible blue shoes, I have to see day and night.

Looking upon them, I want them gone and now!

Thoughts cross my mind frequently each day:

The blender, a dog, a paper shredder or fire;

All ways to take those horrific blue shoes away!

Break Through

. . . .

Silently the shadows lurk

Just beyond the wall of thought;

And violence caged

Is restless to break the bonds upon it.

A matter of time is all that stands

Between the inevitable, and now.

She Did It Again

Lower and lower

Her wickedness does go

Far below the depths of her own

Views of a religious hell.

Sabotage and betrayal

Are what I feel when I hear

Her latest attempt to ruin lives,

And hurt an innocent.

My own small boy

Finally with me, for some time away,

A trip to another coast

With and to his true and loving family.

From his mouth,

The truth of her evil is told

In the words of a three year old,

Unaware of his words, only repeating what he was told.

"I don't have to listen; aunt V told me so,"

"I don't have to do anything; aunt V told me so,

She said it's good to ignore mommy."

And so the words go on . . .

"I don't wanna eat! Aunt V said not to while on the trip"

"I need to get little on the trip so aunt V will be happy."

Each sentence a dagger from a bitter woman,

A bitter woman with no conscience.

How does she sleep with knowledge of how

An innocent boy's mind is tumbled with her poisonous words?

A little boy who has struggled his whole life to gain weight,

She now advises not to eat.

Her own interests at heart,

She hurts the innocents to get her way.

Lying to and manipulating anyone she may choose,

As long as she thinks it will get her, her way.

Self righteous in her actions

As she quotes biblical scripture in her life;

She is hypocritical in her every action and word,

Betraying he, she calls her god.

I could feign surprise at her latest actions,

But the falseness of the surprise would remain apparent.

Time and again she does these things

Showing all the cruelty of her nature.

A Battle Apart

The time I've lost;

The days, the years,

I know I can't get them back.

The people responsible

Should have to answer

For the hurt in both our hearts.

The years of anguish;

Of dreams, nightmares,

And sleepless nights

The days that slowly pass

Marking the hours apart,

For a mother with a broken heart.

And a baby, to be taken from home,

From the love and security he knew,

With no real way to understand.

His heart hurts, and his mind is lost,

Trying to comprehend

What happened to his life.

And years pass, as a desperate mom

Fights with everything she has

To see her son, and bring him home.

But around each turn there is a stop,

Another dead end to her quest

And another hopeless night.

When friends step in, binding together

To help this young mom and her son,

Things slowly turn a little brighter.

The battle still wages

And her son is not yet home,

But the loving mom, still fights on.

Days of Peculiar

The drawn out fight

Causing so much wrong

Taking such a positive turn.

Then a voice from the past

With the words I've waited to hear

Speaks straight to me.

Now on the edge

Of all things sane

An owl stops me in the street.

The camel in my mind

Is becoming over burdened with

Each little straw

Being placed on the heap.

The fight isn't over,

In truth I'm only halfway through

And each morning I wake

To face the daily struggle.

The voice though sweet

And seemingly sincere

Knows not the mess he unwittingly enters.

And the owl, his eyes never leaving me,

Flew away.

Part II:

Relationships

Intrigue

Interest

Long look

Brows raised

Mouth curved.

Glance away

Eyes down,

Then back,

At him.

At First Sight

Eyes, an ever changing hue;

Intriguing green, and innocent blue,

Silently staring back at you.

Sweet pink lips, curve up in a smile.

And wishing time would stop awhile,

You remove your jaw from the tile.

Cheeks flushed and eyes aglow,

Her smile spreads, sweet and slow.

What she's thinking, you'll never know.

Tempting

Daring and tempting

There's nothing casual

About her appeal

Legs for miles

And lips for sin

She's trouble and yet

You long for a kiss

A cunning mind

Shines in her eyes

A mere look

Will draw you in

Her stately lines

Draw the eye

Her sweet smile

Draws your heart

You want closer

To smell and feel

Her hair and skin

The small of her back

And slender waist

The perfect shape

For hands to claim

To wrap around

She's built to please

To tempt and tease

One long look

Can bring a man

To his knees

First Kiss

A tentative touch,

Testing, tasting,

He searches for a response;

An answer to the question,

To go on, or to stop.

Met with no resistance,

The play goes on.

With lips touching

She reaches for him,

To steady her world

That is now off balance.

Holding him

As an anchor to this world,

That has begun to spin;

As she registers

This new sensation,

Of blissfulness.

Still at first,

Absorbing the moment,

She moves to participate.

Slowly giving in

To the need to let go,

To release control.

Silently he gives

Gentle encouragement

To go on,

But she draws back;

Awash in fear,

Afraid of the unknown,

And the unexpected feelings

It brings.

She regains her rigidity,

Her composure and control,

Schooling her features

To reflect a calm

She does not feel.

Her mind wanders

As she refuses to admit

How shaken she was

By her first kiss.

Second Chance

It seems the world

Has seen it fit

To grant me one request.

A future of peace

And a present of happiness

With one unlike the rest.

His is the face

I'd always hoped to see

When I got my wish.

The symmetry and lines

That make up his face

Have always been the best for me.

His heart is pure

With a smile so sweet

His company each day

Sweeps me off my feet.

One More Chance

. . . .

I didn't want to,

But I thought about you.

A lot.

All of the things you've said,

All that has eventually led,

To this.

The memories of times that were good

Don't block out the bad like they should,

Not yet.

With worries and fear, I take a chance . . .

On you, on love, and the memory of a dance,

That night.

Let's do this right, another chance,

To put each other above

All else.

Sunrise

On a new day

On a fresh beginning

The sun will rise.

With the sun

My love will rise

Never to fall

With the setting sun.

Brilliantly rising

Above the world

In your hands and heart

My love will soar.

With you my love,

The world is light

Full of love and possibilities

In your arms.

The sun only rises

On a better day, each day,

That we spend entwined;

Our hearts and minds

And entire lives

Together ensconced.

Curled up together,

Forever more,

To watch the rising sun.

Behind Glass

Countless times I've traced the lines

The curves and angles of your face;

Once filled with warmth and life

Now only glass for my fingers to trace.

Your eyes now don't change, their color

And the gold in them remain, your expression constant.

Your lips, now a memory, forever framed;

I trace them most, contemplate moving on, but I can't.

The memory of their soft touch

Brings my hand to my lips in remembrance;

Never will I forget your first kiss

Walking that night on the way to a dance.

In this frame, behind this glass,

Your face still smiles, but not at me.

I was not there, on that trip taken in spring,

And though it's been many years since I've seen you,

To love you forever, I am free.

Coming Down From the Clouds

Ten years of wanting and waiting
For the moment that never came.
Wanting to step down from the plane
And into your embrace;
Over a decade past, and I still feel the same.

Nerves of anticipation
Dance along my spine
As excitement tingles in my toes.
The smile of joy has not left my face
As the butterflies in my stomach
Throw a party of their own.

After all these years, and countless dreams,
Will I finally get my moment?
Will I be in your arms
When this plane comes down from the clouds?

My worries are real,
And as present as my smile,
As I await the possibility of my dreams coming true.

Your Face in Sleep

. . . .

How can mere words describe

The beauty of your face?

Sweeping brows dash across

The smooth expanse of your forehead

That creases with each raise and furrow of those brows

That so nicely shadow your hypnotizing eyes.

So brown at times they appear all black

They shift to gold one fleck at a time,

Until your joy is shining through

The deepest amber of the earth, deeply veined in gold.

Your lashes dance across those eyes

With each blink your eyelids take in their attempt to awake.

I can feel the world sitting in wait

For the warmth of your gaze to again appear,

Its fire bringing to life all that was once cold.

Your nose is proof that pure adorable

Only adds to beauty and perfection;

Its form and shape of strait lines and angles

With the cutest curves of all; complimenting all,

As it meets the planes that make up your face.

The angle of your cheeks

Change with each passing moment

To alter your look and broadcast

Your feelings, thoughts, and moods.

They extend to your strong stubborn jaw line,

That draws both my eyes and my fingertips.

As you wake I am then drawn

To the wonder that is your lips;

Now gracing me with your first smile of the day

And the sun rises.

My own lips move to greet you good morning

When their true desire is to meet yours in a kiss.

A single finger blows me a kiss

And my lip is bit in response.

I envy that finger's touch of your lips;

I know their feel—living silk beneath my wandering fingertips,

And heaven pressed to my lips,

Your smile captivates my attention

From your lips to your sparkling eyes;

Every line on your face speaks to me

In ways no other can understand.

I love your face and all its intricacies,

But it is the soul beneath it, giving it its light,

That I truly love the most.

Your Beautiful Body

Soulful eyes,

Full of experience

And emotion,

Staring in them,

I easily get lost.

Broad shoulders,

And two strong arms,

You can easily lift me,

And wrap around me

To keep me warm.

The softest hands,

Smooth but strong,

I love their feel,

On my skin.

Your beautiful chest

Tapers down

To those sexy masculine hips,

Each one begging

To be bit, oh so gently.

Long legs,

And a shapely behind,

Are part of the package,

That I'll gladly keep.

Even your feet,

Some might overlook,

But me, I'll rub them,

And put you to sleep.

Your body is so beautiful,

I love to stop and stare.

And the biggest of smiles

Comes over my face,

When I remember the best part:

It's all mine.

Admired

The inviting curve of his back

Calls my hands to trace the line;

While the swell of his shoulders,

So defined in muscle,

Just beg to be admired.

The length of his legs, travel up,

Leading my eyes to his very well defined back side.

He is art, pure and simple,

Without even seeing his face.

Bliss

Locked in passionate embrace,

The sweetest smile on my face.

Our love and fire takes us high

And burns ever brighter.

But here in the aftermath,

Is the purest of joy,

And the sweetest of pleasures.

Lying here with you,

So pleased with our passion spent,

Forever looks so peaceful,

For as long as I am in your heart

And in your arms.

The Beauty of a Face

The chill of glass greets my fingers
As I trace the curves of your face.
I could draw you with a blindfold on,
So well I know your handsome face.

My mind has painted a thousand pictures
Of your many looks throughout the years
But none that I have ever imagined
Could come close to the look you give me.

Poetry, for centuries, has been composed
To tell the beauty of a person or face;
No words, then or now, could ever do justice
To the beauty and wonder I see in your eyes.

I do not get lost in your eyes,
In your eyes I am found;
Our minds and souls truly are one
In two bodies wandering this earth.

I may try forever to put the right words in order

To describe your beauty inside and out,

And if ever I succeed, I know they won't be enough

And they will not do justice to the vows I try to write.

How I feel for you has no known words,

No way to describe in linear thought;

In my search for words, to somehow describe,

I come up quite empty handed each time.

Three words come out; they don't say enough,

They are all I have for now, but I will find more.

I love you, my dear, my darling, divine,

I love you, John, forever be mine.

Chance

So many thoughts,

So many people,

So many possibilities,

What is the chance

That I would find

And love you?

So many options,

So many choices,

So many chances,

What is the chance

That you would

Choose and love me?

No matter it all,

You found me,

And I choose you,

To love and be with

Now and ever more.

Winter Love

Framed in fire

Fueled in desire

The night goes on

In each other's arms.

The fire blazing

Lights a darkened room,

Shadows dancing

Light flickering,

And the flames

They seem to be licking

The two bodies before it.

Years Past

Years ago, on this very day,
I met the man who would become
The center of my world.

You caught my eye, from across the room,
And to this day my eyes smile at the sight of you.
You made me smile back then, and I am smiling still,
With each passing day I love you more than the day I fell.

The memories we made I want to keep forever,
And I want us to make many more in the years to come.

We had our problems along the way,
But they were not enough to keep us apart.
Our love stayed strong, and we returned to each other
With the help of a little well placed courage.

We are together now, and forever more,
Planning our future in each other's arms.
I want to celebrate you, my love,
Making each day better than the last.

I See

. . . .

You wonder what I see in you, but you should rest assured;

I see the world and all of its possibilities

And a love that has lasted forever, all when I look in your eyes.

I see promises made, then put on hold, but never were they gone;

I see love and happiness, devotion and hope,

A future of joy, and a life set to always get better.

I've dreamt for years of having your heart,

To fill the place left by my own when I gave it to you.

Years of trying to fill the space left empty all those years

Never amounted to much at all,

Memories of you have always been stronger

They override all else; capturing my heart in their wake

And holding my mind in the past.

My Heart

My heart

My love

My valentine

I love you dearly, above all else.

With you my heart is overflowing

In your arms I find bliss.

My life is not calm,

My heart is not steady,

But in your arms I find peace,

And perfect contentment.

You hold my heart, my Valentine,

You are my love, for all of time.

May Day

May Day is here, and I am for you;

All my heart, and all my love,

Forever are yours to keep.

Hold them and me with tender passion;

Always protecting, always caring,

And always loving me too.

If this promise, you can keep,

I'll ask you to be mine,

Forever entwined,

Our two hearts together,

And your hand in mine.

I Am Amazed By You

Your mind intrigues me, and your thoughts are provoking;

Your love and compassion takes my breath away.

Your face is still poetry, unspoken in my mind,

And your words are sweeter than the ripest strawberry.

I find I want you more and more each day.

Each picture makes me want to see, every inch of you in person;

Each word on the phone, I long to hear your voice in my ear;

And every silence, I want to be shared together.

Pictures of your body now never escape my mind,

And my hands have their own mind

As they dream of holding yours.

My own body is a traitor

Ignoring the logic of my mind

Wanting yours as it does.

Years went by, with you in my mind

And forever is how long you've been in my heart;

Others come and go, passing through life,

But eternally your presence remained.

Now every word provokes a longing

To bring our hearts together;

And every day brings us closer

To a future I can only guess.

Just Us Two

It's a glowing warmth

From deep within

Your eyes are the start

Of the feelings that are stirring

And melt my heart.

Your look, a glance,

Of energy and love;

Your touch, a caress,

Of comfort and reassurance.

I love you more than

Anything in this world,

My darling heart,

My sweet man,

My true love.

Forever us two,

Forever me and you

That is my wish . . .

For our end

And our start,

My darling mine,

My darling heart.

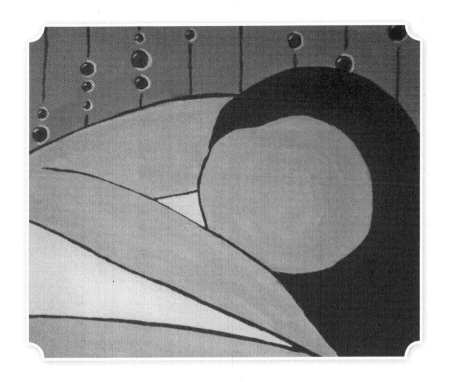

Devoted

. . . .

True devotion

Eternal and evermore

My one and only,

You have my heart.

In your arms I am home,

In your life I am happy.

There can never be another,

I want you now and ever more,

My love.

Good Night

Good night my king, till I awake,
And the sun once more graces your face.

Sleep well and deep, my darling mine,
Dream of the day our limbs may entwine.
In blissful slumber, curled up in you,
Truly happy slumber, our whole lives through.

When dawn arrives to brighten our eyes
I'll awake to find you by my side.

If I awake to find instead an empty place
Where I dreamt you were resting your face,
Then I shall close my eyes a moment more
And picture you there, so my heart may soar.

Sleeping alone when I want you near
Will never be satisfactory, I fear.

Turmoil

What Is Love?

What is love to me?

An emotion?

A commitment?

Or a compromise?

I'm not sure

If it's one, all, or other,

But I consider it often.

Should there be a difference,

Between the love for family and romantic love?

Shouldn't your romantic love

Join and become your family?

Then why do they seem like such opposites?

My Life in Full Circle

I have been here before,

Not this house, not this date,

But definitely here.

I started out with you,

Then I moved on, and out,

A different direction.

I find myself back again.

Changed My Mind

He spoke of things

That he did not keep,

He lied and tricked

And spoke no more of it.

Thanks to that,

My opinion has changed

No longer is he viewed as trusting and honest,

Now each time I see him,

There are doubts surrounding every word.

Trust is easy to lose,

And so difficult to gain back.

My mind has shadowed him,

And he will no longer have my trust.

All it takes is that one little lie,

That in another's eyes is not so little,

To ruin an opinion,

That was once so good.

Are You Missed? Am I?

Do I miss you

Or do I miss us?

Is it loneliness

Or a new chapter?

Am I losing you

Or finding me again?

I miss your company,

I long for your touch,

And I fear in my absence

You'll find another,

And not need me.

Emotionally and physically

I'm entwined in you,

But are you as tangled in me?

When You Were Mine

Time to realize

Nothing is free

Even these memories

Cost a little of me.

The life I had

When you were mine,

Is in my heart

And always on my mind.

So wrapped up in you,

On anything, I was sold.

I never wanted us to end

Until your heart grew cold.

Now I sit here in the dark

With endless longing in my heart

For the happiness we once knew

And the love I still feel for you.

Not a Chance

It wasn't the 'no'

That saddened me,

Nor was it that we disagreed.

It was the chance.

You didn't give it one.

The idea,

Could have been something to discuss,

To think about further,

Something we decided together.

Instead it was shot down,

Without a chance,

Not even a moment

Of consideration.

Why is that?

Talk To Me

Talk to me

My darling love

Let us communicate,

Work it out,

And smile again.

We know ourselves

Good and bad,

Ups and downs,

Living each day

Learning to share,

To get along,

Loving each other.

So let's talk

My darling love

And stay together

Our arms entwined

A long embrace

A lasting love

Based on talk.

No Apology

I forgive the mistakes,

But I'll never forget,

The mess you made,

And the way you left me in the middle of it all.

Some things should not need said,

Some things should be known.

Life is in no way easy,

But it is also not that hard.

To do what you have done,

To be the way you are,

You see nothing wrong,

So you offer no apology.

But you mistake me,

For your careless ex,

I do care,

And I am not pleased.

I do not over look things as she did,

I do not let such major things

Just slide on by.

But just because I am more responsible

Than the two of you put together,

Does not mean I want the weight of the world

Placed on my shoulders,

And my shoulders alone.

Linger

. . . .

I should simply

Forget and let go,

But my mind refuses

And I dwell on it daily.

Why does something like this

Bug me so?

I do not know,

But I can't just let it go.

Wrong

It wasn't right

That passion they shared

A night together

Lost in thoughts of another.

A sense of betrayal

Wanting to take it back

Those moments of lust

Not right, in the morning light.

Not even right in the moment,

They did it anyway,

Ignoring the feeling of how wrong.

You're Online

Profiles and nicknames,
All sluts and whores,
Yet you want all them
But never me.

I was there
For two whole years,
Wanting your love,
Needing your attention,
Yet I was ignored.

I finally stepped out,
For a life of my own,
For some thing I never had from you.

You turned to them,
After years of ignoring me;
I had thought you young,
Or just not mature in that way,
But the second I am gone,
You become an online whore.

Every site,

Designed for sex,

A booty call,

And one night stands.

You had a wife,

Loving and caring,

Yet you wanted nothing of her,

Nothing of me.

I thought it just did not appeal,

That you might not be that into sex,

But as it turns out,

I was the fool,

You just weren't into me.

In this age of computers,

I guess you didn't need a wife in your life.

So I won't be there again,

Never to keep you away from the life you chose.

I am free,

As are you,

To go our own ways,

As I see you have chosen yours.

Lonely

With you I was lonely,

Set apart, and left alone.

Day to day, you left,

Leaving me there,

In a home that was not a home,

Without thought each day

What could I do but wait,

And live in lonesome,

Until you come back,

And I end up more alone

Than I was when you were gone.

You do your thing

Paying no heed to me,

I am the living ghost,

Going in and out

Of the rooms in your house.

Appreciated

I need to feel it, and to hear it,

And to see it in your eyes.

So many days

All I wanted was a thank-you,

A kiss when you walk in the door,

A hug when I needed comfort,

And a re-assurance

When things seem out of hand.

I do so much for you,

Day to day

I want you happy,

But don't I deserve

The same in return?

Violet

Why can't he see

The hurt he causes in me

To let her go

When I want I her so.

And knowing I'll miss her

Does nothing to deter;

I'll see her still

Up to the day until

I can see her no more,

And my heart will be sore.

But I'd rather see her and miss her,

Than avoid her, and the pain,

That losing her will bring.

I don't really know,

Why the connection is so strong,

Or why I'm so drawn

To a little girl like her.

But she seems so right,

So perfect for me.

He has one of his own,

So what is so wrong with mine?

I don't fully understand

But perhaps that's because I'm so involved.

For really I know

Now is not the best time

To bring home such a cute little dog.

But then again,

Is there really a right time,

For any thing in life?

I guess I only complain,

Because I like her so much,

And being around her

Makes me happy,

Even when it's only for awhile.

I'll sure miss her when she's gone,

My cute little Violet, girl.

How can I tell him,

What I really want,

When I know he doesn't

Want her at all?

I want us to talk,

And on most things,

We do.

So why is this subject

So hard to bring up,

And always so short a talk?

So silly a question,

I know the answer,

It is his point of view.

I bring up the possibility,

He sees only the negative,

And mentions them at every turn.

I see them too,

But there must be a way,

To make it work for all.

To have it all,

And still keep the happiness

And the love,

That I live with now.

So I wait and wonder

Silent most of the time,

Awaiting what life,

Will hand me next.

Writing it down,

Putting words to paper

Brings out the emotions

I try each day to hide.

The sadness above all,

Grips me quite hard

But no matter the strength

I refuse to give in

To those tears just waiting,

Below my shaky surface.

Instead I will stop this writing,

And search for better thoughts.

I'll visit my Violet,

And she'll lift my spirits

As she's done so many days

That I just love her company.

But what will I do when she is gone?

Do I Hate You?

I cannot say for sure

If I truly hate you

Or just what you've done.

Hatred is so strong,

Will my soul allow it?

If so,

Would my mind accept it?

I think not.

I do not feel you are a bad person,

Merely not a considerate one.

You never considered me all through marriage,

You did not consider your actions

Nor their consequences.

You did not consider your son,

The angel you damned to hell.

You did not consider my feelings

When you started down this path.

What do you consider yourself?

Compromising Relationship

You say I don't compromise,

And that you've compromised too much,

So it must not be obvious

What I give up for you.

First and foremost is time.

Every minute I spent trying to make it work,

The times I spent with you

Instead of with others,

Who needed me so much more.

Even now as I sit here

And you've driven away,

I see how little my time means,

To someone such as you.

My cat is another

Sacrifice made for you,

And never once did you even say thank you

For the pain and loss I have gone through

Tucker was my baby
Before I had my son.
A sweet and loving companion,
But I had to leave him for you,
No cats allowed in your house,
Your control is always important to you.

Comfort, in the most basic sense
Is not found, coming home each day.
I freeze.
I tell you this, but you don't care,
The thermostat is yours.
Even when I was paying the bill,
The thanks I got,
Was a cold body, and numb feet.

Another to add, my right to breathe.
Crazy though it may sound,
This too has been on shaky ground.
You walk in a room, I cough and gag,
Holding my breath until I can leave.
The smell you carry around,
The residue of your bad habit,
Makes me bury my nose in my sleeve.

Again I tell you, but you tell me,

You must be in control.

My friends, they too, have had to go

Your suspicious mind could not handle

A girl like me, talking to and being around

Friends of the opposite gender.

What next, I ask, will be too much?

Stating my opinion?

Though when I give it, I'm shot down,

Things must go your way, after all.

Like this house, you said it is ours,

Until I have an idea, then it's yours,

Things will be done your way.

During the renovation, I state my opinion on chandeliers.

You put them down, and said no way,

Insisting anything you pick will be better.

A month or so, down the line,

You buy them, and I think you sweet,

But you make it clear, you didn't do it for me.

They were on sale, and quite a deal,

You just couldn't let me believe.

My daily routine, a trip to the gym, sure you went a few times.

But after a few, it doesn't suit you,

And I can't change your mind.

But on top of that, you dislike me going alone,

Though I've done it for years, before I met you.

So in the end, I give it up,

Else face the consequences, you say.

And the time I wanted Violet,

A sweet little dog, who I loved so much.

This I figured would be a compromise,

I gave up my cat for you,

And you already have your dog, what is the harm in two?

I went to that shelter, and saw her each day,

While waiting for you, to make your call.

In such a tough time,

When I needed love, a friend, and a distraction,

You told me no, even when I begged.

I went on thinking of her

And wishing she was mine,

Even after the day, someone else took her away.

My clothes, they too, changed for you,

Some now are even gone.

Most were those, I got from my mom.

The foods I like, and used to eat most,
You ruled out without a thought.
Then I eat what you like best,
Whether I like it or not.
Some, I'll say, I like it now,
But my taste buds had to be taught.

You see none of this in your rage,
As you drive off and away.
I'm left here, as you say, I too,
Need space to think this through.

I've been thinking, for some time now
Of what I'm going through,
But the problem I see isn't as easy
As whether I think of you.

More to truth, the problem stands
At whether you consider me.
Do you notice what I do for you,
And will you ever truly see?

Labor of Love

It's a labor of love, being with you

Each moment a mixture, of love and pain.

The confusion of a mind, so tumbled in thoughts

So lost in possibilities of past, present, and future.

Dilemmas arise, each passing day

Problems so large, lives hang in the balance,

the chances and choices stand endless

in long procession, beyond immediate reach.

But happiness now, could possibly lead

To hurt and harm in years to come.

So do we stay in peace, with future war,

Or leave the war, never to come

Leaving the happiness, also gone?

The problems we face, can be faced alone,

But as a team we grow stronger,

And we gain the chance, to win it all.

Inquiry

Silently I ask

For a loving touch,

A caring look

To reassure me

I'm still the one.

No response for me

Not in my favor

I'm sent away,

Neither love nor company,

Empty handed.

I walk slowly

Leaving the room,

Waiting for the hope

A second glance can bring,

But it never comes.

In Your World

I'm set at a distance

Never to get near

In a world of strangers,

I just need a friend.

Set apart, and sent away,

Each time that I draw near,

You back away,

And I am put in my place.

Apart from you

And far from your heart

Your soul I simply can't understand

I am kept too far away.

You stay there,

In your world

Out of my loving embrace

That is offered, but pushed away.

I want closeness,

Comfort and caring,

Two people in love,

Giving and sharing.

So why do I stay

To be treated this way?

Set aside and ignored

As you go on your own way?

Because it is my heart that loves

And cares for you,

Wishing on, for the closeness I need

But so far, I only find in my dreams.

Eventually Me

So out of place

Sitting here lost

Among your friends

I don't fit in

No real surprise

Just as before

Each crowd I meet

They're fine enough,

Just not for me.

I just agree,

Go where you like

Always trying

To please you

And not me.

I guess it's time

To stop pretending,

Accept, I'm me,

But not just yet.

A Decision Made . . . . By Both Sides of the Brain

. . . .

Left alone,	to think and ponder,
My mind,	now so calm and clear,
And soul,	all that makes up me,
Now know,	what I want and need.

My life,	and its twists and turns,
Can be,	with some hope and change,
Made new,	mistakes all righted,
In time,	things will go my way.

I will,	work to right the wrongs,
Now do,	all the things I must,
What I,	have been putting off,
Have to,	now face the hard truth.

The Man in You

I was hurt by you
Deep in my heart

I felt betrayed by you
When you pushed us apart.

I told them all
Each person who asked,

That I never loved you,
That I was glad I packed.

But I lied to them,
And to myself, you see,

Because leaving you
Was hardest on me.

Through your angry childishness
I saw the man I loved within,

But I could not stay there

And not pay attention

To the jealousy I saw each day

And the anger boiling up inside.

I could not live with you, in fear,

Seeing all that, and wanting to hide.

So instead I left

And I did not look back,

Though our love was still there,

It was compassion you lacked.

Your patience had worn thin,

And your understanding had flown away

In my attempts to talk to you,

There was nothing I could say.

So I told the world

You were bad for me,

That I had made the wrong choice,

And that I was blind, and could not see.

But what I could see,
Hurt most of all.

Deep under the mess you had become
Was the man I knew you could be.

And it was that man,
That I never wanted to leave,

And though I wouldn't admit it,
It was what made me believe

That in time you would grow
Filling with love to the seams,

Until one day you'd once more be,
Close to perfection,

To the one man I still measure all the rest against;
The man I see in my dreams.

Last Kiss

We never saw it coming
The end that came so soon
Sudden darkness in the night
The setting of the moon

Speaking of forever
Never dreaming of this
We never saw it coming
The start of our last kiss.

I can remember the day
The night I truly knew
The depth of my feelings
The love I felt for you

You made the difference
Between night and day
Not once had we expected
Those feelings to slip away

Though we didn't know
It would lack the old bliss

Each of us will remember

The day we had our last kiss

The day I noticed your kiss

Only brought me sorrow

The day that showed me sadly

There would be no kisses tomorrow

Without You

I'm locking doors,

Doing things alone,

And passing time.

I'm hugging pillows,

Talking to walls,

And counting days.

Soon counting weeks,

Now it is months,

But do I really miss you?

I am happy with me,

And relationships are sweet,

But at times I wonder

If I am better

On my own,

Or as a pair.

But no matter how sweet

Being a pair can be,

With the wrong person,

It is also agony.

Memories of You

Yearning and longing

To see your sweet face

So familiar yet different

New marks of age in place.

I still know your heart,

The kindness in your soul,

It shines in the darkness

Of my own heart, filling the space.

The desire to see you

To speak your name,

Though I know if I do,

It would never be the same.

But the longing is still there

And I still have that wish

For one more caring hug,

And one more sweet kiss.

My memories of you

Have attention, well paid,

And though time passes,

Those moments never fade.

I still move on from the foundation

Of hurt and distrust you have laid,

But I know my thoughts

And those moments, will never fade.

Claim to Change

I loved you so much

When the pain came I ran

How could my love

Hurt me that way?

Time moved on and so did I

So when old friends asked

What happened with you,

I smile and say it's not my business to know.

I told myself, I was glad you were gone

That I was better because of it.

I had my days when I missed you

But I remembered the hurt, and got on with my day.

You tell me now, you've changed your ways

That you are better than before

A part of my heart wants to believe you

But my mind and the rest of me are screaming NO!

Sour Second Chances

Starting out so good at first,

Smooth sailing and happy smiles.

But the changes he promised did not exist,

Fights from the past came back to haunt,

And slowly it looked not worth the risk.

As history repeats, we end up just as we were.

Now warning bells will chime

When a second chance is presented next time.

Now I'm moving on, and throwing second chances to the wind.

Because though at first they bring a smile

It only lasts that one short while.

Then it ends, as it must,

With more doubt than there is trust.

From now on go with some one new,

Not some one bound to get strike two.

Family

Family Away

For years I have been apart
From parts of my family
For reasons I am not sure.

My world has fallen astray
Many have come together
My family included.

Older siblings gone so long
Often remembered in thoughts
Of parties and holidays.

Wondered about at my own
Wedding for sure, I really
Wanted my family there.

Part of me hopes all the time
Pieces lost over time, bring
Peace when we come together.

A Sister or Not?

I am an older sister,

But am I?

I am a younger sister,

But am I?

My younger sister and I

Have been raised as one,

With no real distinction

In age between us.

So I am not a role model,

Nor a symbol in

My own little sister's life.

My older sister left so young,

And I was even younger;

My memories, though strong,

Have changed

With the time that has past.

I did not really get the chance,

To be the little sister.

I am a sister to two sisters,

But really,

What kind of sister am I?

A Lifetime Apart

A single picture of you

Is all I have, from an article done years ago

For the military in Iraq.

I want to know you,

To see you in person, as you are a part of me

Long since departed.

Family is so dear to me,

To be apart is so difficult,

But how would I go about bridging the gap?

So long has passed

So much has changed,

And silence has stretched on through these years.

The impersonal internet could lend a hand,

A phone number, I may never call,

Or an address, that is by all means, years out of date.

What do I say to a sister or brother

That left when I was so young?

Hello, I do not know you, but I do.

Nonsense to my own ears, and certainly to theirs,

But I do want to know them,

Even just a little.

Family is, after all,

So important and necessary

So much a part of me, that I dream about a bridge.

From a small piece of wood,

To elaborate decorative metal structures,

Bringing my family all together,

After all this time.

Am I the bridge, or just standing on one side of it?

Who Are My Parents?

Who really knows their own parents?

Are they the fairytale characters we make them in our minds?

Or people just like we have grown into ourselves?

I have spent so many years idealizing perfection

In the way I viewed my own parents,

But now I am firm in my belief that they are not perfect,

But they are amazing people who have done their best in life

Like I am currently trying to do as well.

I have had so many questions,

That remain unanswered about my family and my past.

My older siblings, and the stories there,

I have only been able to take what I know,

And guess about the rest.

My parent's relationship, and how it is when I am not looking,

Is it really as wonderful as it looks to the outside eye?

I may never know the history as fully as I would like,

Or the details that my questing mind craves,

But at least I know without a doubt,

That the love I have for them is very strong and very true,

Unshakable by any event in this life or the next.

The Meet

Meeting you

After years gone past

Wanting to know you,

To reconnect.

Words spoken,

Trusting,

I believed every word.

Finding later

The truth was missing.

Why this is so,

I do not know.

I wanted only family,

A connection broken

From the past.

Instead there are stories:

Complex,

Well thought out fiction,

Of which the author in me

Should be proud.

But in them instead

I find disappointment.

I was not looking for fiction,

I was in search of family and truth.

Lacking the latter,

I'm left to wonder:

Is there hope for the first?

Part III:

Moments and People

A Motorcycle Ride

The roar of the engine

Drowns my thoughts

The open road

Calls my mind,

And away from my body

It flies.

Down winding roads

At a speed I can't read,

My spirit flies.

Spring Dance

Butterflies, dragonflies, and weeds

Sway in the morning breeze,

Bringing in the serenity of spring

Slowly approaching from the south.

The wind tosses them playfully,

A dance of freedom and joy;

Circling the bright yellow wild flowers .

Scattered amongst the grass and weeds.

Joy

Eyes down cast

Reading a book

In his own little world.

He restrains his laughter

. In this public setting,

But the smile of joy

Remains on his face,

And reaches his eyes.

When the smile leaves,

It's never gone for long.

As he reads the next passage,

The corners of his mouth

Flick up in almost a smile

From the pleasure of his book.

More laughter,

No longer restrained

With a flash of teeth,

And a warm smile

He displays his enjoyment

Over the written word,

Never even caring

If others watch or see.

When his hand comes up

To cover another laugh,

The enjoyment can still be seen

Shining from his eyes,

Showing off the lines

Winking at the corners

From years of laughter before.

A Concerned Look

. . . .

Frowning over the screen

He shakes his head.

The typing has paused,

And he exhales loudly.

Turning a page

He tries to move on

But concentration pulls him

To complete the first.

Brows furrowed,

He sets back to work,

The computer again clicking away.

Chocolate

It sits tempting me

Colorful wrapping

Adorned with a bow

Teasing me

Dark and milky caramel

Individually wrapped

I'll just sneak one

Don't tell,

Crowded Talk

People

Gather

Voices

Mingle

Questions

Answers

Talk

Continues

Eyes

Dart

Watching

Glance

Away

Postures

Change

Adjust

Shifting

Relax

Mouths

Move

Shaping

Words

Smiling

Friendly

Banter

Conversations

Laughter

Chaos

Voices mingle

Taking place of sense

Each talking to another

None to me.

Faceless faces

Pressing bodies

Jumbled words

Languages apart.

People moving

A door slams

Above the sound

Of the clamoring crowd.

Much Needed Time Away

The white in my hair
And the new lines in my face
Clearly state
That I need a break.

People and events
Have been working overtime
To wear me down,
Past my reserves.

So off on a plane
I flew away,
Just me and my boy;
A short escape of our own.

Time away
Visiting family and friends
For some fun and distraction
From the mess I left behind.

Airports

How can I explain

The change in me

When I enter an airport?

Whether by plane or car

I arrive as me.

The longer I stay

My mind fragments;

Quotes from long ago

Repeat in my mind

Causing me to search the crowd,

"Don't be surprised

If I'm there at the airport

The very moment you land;

I've missed you so much

Don't be surprised

If I swim the ocean

To be sure I'm there."

So many words

Around these and others

Causing my mind to forget

Why I am there now,

And instead becomes a tool of my youth.

My eyes scan the faces,

Of only the men

And my foolish heart

Still hopes to see you.

Why this is,

I may never know,

For that moment you spoke of

Was gone long ago.

It has not helped

That my subconscious is also a traitor

To my every waking thoughts,

As it dreams over and over

Of the reunion I was deprived

At an airport such as this one.

Hunger

A driving need

A constant disturbance

Never to cease

Until the call is answered.

Deep throbbing pains

And a one track mind,

until the desire is sated.

A primal urge,

A driving pull,

That will never end

And never let you rest,

Until the hunger is abated.

Get Away

A day away

A day to myself

To get away

And let troubles melt

When life gets complex

And trouble lined

I just need a break

And time to unwind

Finding time

For casual talk

Or finding peace

In a book or a walk

I cherish the times

I get out on my own

Spending time with myself

Yet never alone

Puzzle

One page at a time

My mind will wander

Down the winding pathways

Of my life.

One at a time

The pieces fall into place

In dreams and in life,

It all comes together,

Only to fall apart again.

Who Told Me

I know,

Je sais,

Is the answer to all

Who told me,

You'll never know.

I don't really know it all,

I just find out before you.

I'll finish your sentences

And answer the questions

Yet to be asked.

Its easy for me,

But it amazes you . . .

You don't have to tell me,

Je sais,

I already know.

Visit for a Day

Random day and friendly visit

Someone I haven't seen in so long.

Greetings and smiles, we talk awhile.

Time has passed, changing all but you

As if it were days, not several years since we've been in the same

room.

You have grown up, but change, you have not.

A little slice of my past came alive, and at the sight of you, I smiled.

We spent our time in fun and laughter,

Before I drove away, with my pictures, to my future down the road.

I waved to my friend,

Taking my memories along for the ride.

Relive the Past a Moment

A charming break to relive

The fun and games of my past

A pause in the normal

But only a moment,

It cannot last.

Your Dance

Intense concentration

And pure joy,

Intent eyes

And a furrowed brow,

Then a smile so bright

I have to smile, too.

Seeing you in play,

I know what you feel.

That court is yours,

Like the dance floor is mine.

The movements

Are as natural to you,

As the steps and turns

Are to me.

This is your dance,

And I can only watch

As you travel the court

Moving each muscle

In graceful turn,

To a dance I get to only observe.

Your dance.

Music in the Air

Rhythm and beats resounding in time

The words come later, sweet lyrics of rhyme

The drums are beating their path in the night

While the strings are vibrating light

Each note alone played piece by piece

Soon put together as the tempos increase

When the music stops the conversation around is a bore

I find I miss the notes that filled the room only moments before.

Perfect Day

A day of joy, of passion and peace

Spent in smiles of work and play

Never knowing one from the other

Too busy enjoying my perfect day.

Children's laughter and mingling voices

All a melody to my ears

As I drive home, dreaming of tomorrow

Yet lost in the moment on a day so clear.

Windows down and the radio on

Feeling free to sing along

Every word, a cry of joy

As I sing my favorite songs.

The Girl of My Dreams

Pleasant slumber; I see her face

Framed by a halo of silken hair.

She is a part of me; she holds my heart

Just as my own little one does;

She is the daughter I haven't had.

Time and again she arrests my attention;

A welcome interruption to my subconscious dreams.

An angel without a name; she smiles.

A gentle breeze wakes me with a kiss;

A wistful, wishful smile gracing my own lips.

I've Often Wondered

I've often wondered,

What if . . .

Such an impossible question

With both none, and a million, answers.

But with you, that is all I have;

Endless possibilities with no realities.

How could something that felt so real

Disappear in the blink of an eye

Leaving behind a young girl with her first broken heart

Who grew into a lady; who now questions

Every action in every relationship.

But still I wonder about the first,

That ill-fated relationship that ended too soon.

On that I dwell, and of it I wonder . . .

Dreaming of You

Why are you always on my mind

When I know that you are not mine?

Why cant I stop thinking, of the times that we would sing

Of love and happiness, while in your arms, cuddled up so close?

But now I feel alone, knowing those days are gone

But never truly done

As they play over in my mind

So easy to rewind.

I long for you some days

And the thoughts won't go away.

But do I miss your face

Or the way I felt those days

Wrapped close in your arms

Hoping never to cause you harm

In any way at all

In a situation so confused.

But things went so astray

And I felt I could not stay

While life fell apart around me

It was still only you I'd see

Every night in my dreams

Of life coming apart at the seams.

I may just miss the memories from

Those days of joy, happiness, and more,

But then why do I feel so out of place

On the nights that I don't . . .

Dream about your face.

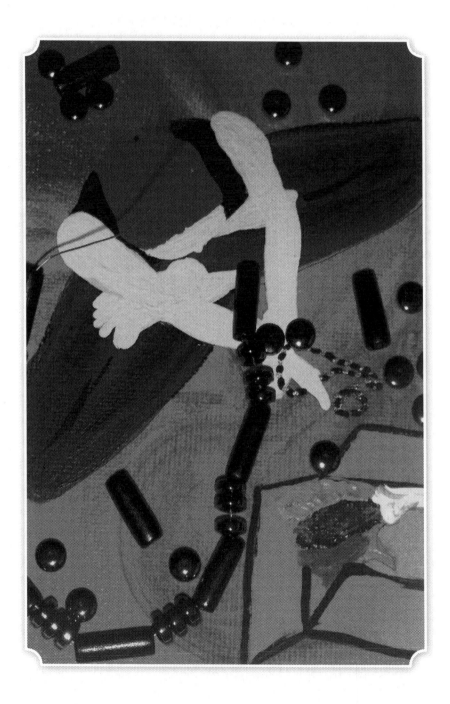

Beads on a String

A piece of the past fell in my lap today
When a box from home arrived for me.
Inside I found, a reminder of you
And the future I might have had.

Beads on a string are all they are,
But they have the power
To bring those memories from afar.

I recall the day I saw these, and picked them out for you,
Looking for another way, to show and say,
How I felt, and how much I thought of you.
Though I have grown, and moved on,
The memories remain.

Beads on a string are all they are,
But they have the power
To bring those memories from afar.

And from there my mind wandered
Into the childish dreams of my past.
A happy marriage after high school,

Starting a family, and a life of love.

Those dreams fell, and left my life;

In their absence I grew, to become

Who I would be in the years to come.

So these beads I'll keep,

Like the memories of my past,

But I'll change them, like myself,

Into an instrument of my future.

Uneventful Day

Hours of nothing surely leads to something;

Sitting in silence, day dreaming away:

Life is a mystery; Why do we stay?

Relax and sit back,

Take a good look around.

Watch the world go by and enjoy

Your uneventful day.

To Live a Dream

Only wishing for a bit of slumber,

To rest my head upon a silken pillow case.

To dream away the night, and the previous day.

But here I remain, sleepless. Forevermore.

Praying that the land of dreams would open up to me,

To explore the depths of a world, more real than my own.

To dare to continue living, in a fantasy world of dreams.

But here I remain, sleepless. Forevermore.

Waking Dream

I woke up today after running into your arms;
Tears streaked my face, when we met in embrace
As I declared to you that, "I could not do it."
Still in the dress picked only for this day,
My arms gripped you tight as the tears flowed free.
I know not who I ran from, or why I ran to you,
But like many dreams before, you met me at the airport
And soothed all that troubled my mind.

I woke up today with the tears still on my face;
The dream so real, I drew the moment.
It left traces of true emotion with me the rest of the day.
After all I have done, and all I have seen,
My mind reverts back to you.
After all I have gone through and the changes that pass,
It seems a part of me will not ever be free.
It is the part I gave freely to you.

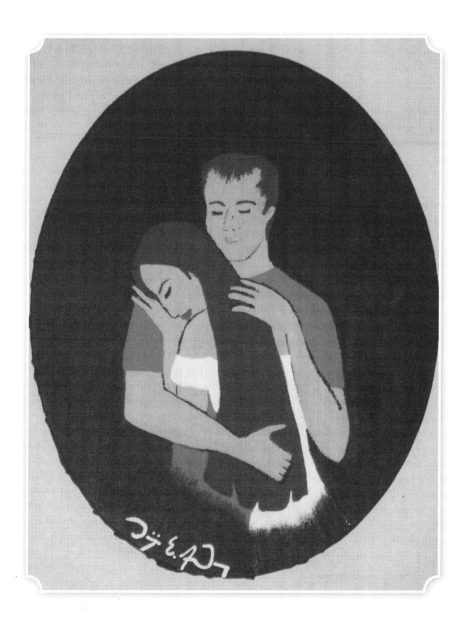

One Thought Too Many

A wild mind will never see rest,

Thoughts tumbling around

Doing their absolute best

To block out all outside sound.

In my mind, the past repeats over and over

And the future takes it's time to linger long.

The present is as lucky as a three leaf clover,

So I think of the future like a fond love song.

My wild mind refuses to sleep,

Each night it is a battle of thoughts and will

Wishes that my mind refuses to silently keep

So in a box they go, to sit on my window sill.

Neatly written, each little wish,

None really so little, but each stashed away

Keeping my mind clear enough to kiss

The day goodnight, and simply lay

My head on my pillow, and finally get some sleep.

If You Could Read My Mind

If you could read my
Wild and crazy mind,

You'd see confusion
And a heart that's kind;

Thoughts full of chaos
Startle and worry

The small part of me
That is still care free.

Dear Friend

You give me strength and courage when mine runs out,

Your hopes and ambition build me up.

Talking to you rebuilds my confidence,

Especially on days my patience is running out.

Thank you my friend for being you,

And for always being there for me.

With out you I do not know where I would be

And what I would be doing right now.

You helped me see, I was not alone

You offered support and help, when I needed it most,

And you gave me love, when I was at my lowest of all.

For all you do and all you are,

I want to say thank you dear friend.

I want to scream it from the mountain tops,

And cry it in your arms,

But most of all I want you to know,

How much you being there has meant to me through it all.

My Guardian Angel

. . . .

When things got dark

And hope was fading

I turned to a smiling face.

A stranger really,

But so filled with warmth,

Compassion and love.

She guided me

When I could not see,

By my side

We became a team

And the odds did not seem so scary.

Through it all

She's been an Angel

Guarding and guiding

No matter the difficulty.

I thank her silently

Everyday

But when I try

To truly express

My appreciation,

I simply cannot find the words to say.

What she has done

Cannot be measured

In time or space,

And surely not in mere words.

And when ever I feel

In my darkest moments,

She saves the day all over again.

Guiding Light

A light in the darkness,

Pointing me towards

The truth and light that seems for so long

Has been buried and out of my reaching grasp.

A man, so wise and caring

Who understands my life and I;

Who does not judge

But listens instead,

And lends a helping hand to my troubles.

He is a kindred sprit,

A kindred soul in this world,

Always advising and aiding me

In my many struggles.

To thank him,

I do not know how,

The gratitude is hard to express.

But no matter the day

Or the time ever,

I count him among my friends,

The few number of trusted and kind people

That make up the support in my life.

Anticipation

Waiting for a minute

Waiting for a moment

Something about to happen

And all you can do is wait.

Knowing what is decided

Can change a lot

You wait in anticipation

For the answer to come.

Never knowing

What the next minute will hold.

Waiting on a moment, waiting on a minute

Each day wondering

What the next second

Will be like.

Silently sitting

Agitation growing

As anticipation rises

At the sight of . . .

Oh the anticipation.

Growing Changes

I am changing

A child no more

The mirror shows

A woman now

With life ahead

So promising.

I've grown beyond

The child I was

I still hold on

To my childhood:

I remember

My up bringing;

Loving parents:

So supportive

Good examples

My role models.

Little sister:

Listens to me

Understands much

Has her own life

Makes time for me.

Little brother:

Always caring

So sweet to all

He's pure at heart.

Relationships:

Each one leading

Time after time

To another

Each one teaching

A new lesson,

Bettering me

Making me grow.

From the young girl

I was before

To the woman

I can now see

In my mirror

Smiling at me

With confidence

And regal grace

Ready to face

Life's challenges

And my changes.

The Crowd of the Lost

Sitting in rows, surrounded by walls,

Covered windows, blocking out light.

Each listening only to what they want to hear,

Each watching and waiting for a sign.

As a preacher informs the lost crowd

That all they do, holds no meaning;

That anything that happens, they can't change.

He speaks in loud tones, punctuating each word or two

With a louder Amen, demanding the lost to repeat.

With every word the crowd of lost

Becomes further lost in the quoting of scripture

That has long since lost its own meaning.

Each person of the lost, are told not to try;

Not to live their lives,

And that there is no need nor point for improvement.

With a confirmation again, of Amen, the lost agree,

Each resting in the idea that they

Need not try anything, nor change anything,

In their mixed up and backwards lives.

Instead of helping this crown to help themselves

The preacher demands they give their souls

To a teacher that long ago died,

And is now overly idolized.

This is not new, though they claim it is,

But I've seen and heard it all before;

Each time in a different tone, a different voice,

But their messages are all the same.

My very being screams against the words I hear,

And the lessons they are loudly preaching.

With relief and thankfulness, it has come,

The time I can leave this backwards place.

I walk out knowing that never will I return.

Mystery

Without words how do they know

The sound of her voice

Or the temper of her being;

With silence comes mystery,

The constant wonder of who and why.

Can she talk, does she speak?

Does she choose silence, is she English?

Is she from some exotic foreign land

Where the waves are bluer and the hills roll on?

Without a word they will never know,

But their imaginations run wild

As they try to guess at the enigma that is

The lady sitting quietly on her own,

Inviting questions, but answering none.

The Wrong Pain

Sense of foreboding

Something not right

Pain deep down

And wrapped around

Every aspect here.

Head to toe

It radiates through

All of me.

This is real,

No dream illusion

Pain is there

On every level

Wearing me out.

Through every inch

Of my being,

A sense of wrong.

I shouldn't hurt

In this way,

Something is wrong.

But what,

I can't say.

Needing help

But not knowing

Where to turn,

I am stuck.

In this pattern,

In this mess,

In this pain.

Control

Every word

Every act

Each planned

In control.

Spontaneity

For others,

Not you

In control.

Shed a tear

A random laugh,

Not here.

Rigid control.

Calculated,

Planned,

No surprises,

Still in control.

Nothing random,

Remain controlled.

Pain

Pain

Aching splitting curling

Wrenching through

Spasming

Spreading tormenting hurting

Pain

Searing swelling mauling

Cutting through

Agonizing

Burning stabbing jolting

Pain.

Crying out in pain

But there is no help.

Acceptance

One day I may fly

Above the voices of this world;

Those of family, strangers, friends,

And the ones that echo in my own mind.

Glancing through this life

I often make the argument

That no one truly knows me,

And no one takes the time to learn.

Now in my constant wandering, I wonder,

Have I ever given anyone a truly fair chance?

Sadly I have come to think not;

For how do you get to know a stranger?

You talk to them, be with them,

And ask all you wish to know.

Now what if that stranger did not know herself?

How could any one, even if they truly desired to,

Get to know the real her?

This is the problem that besets my mind

For many nights now, as I drift off to sleep:

If I do not know nor understand myself,

How can I expect anyone else to know or understand

My many facets and my many flaws?

I try to look within

To see the truth in who I am;

Not the labels the world places upon me,

But the person beneath it all,

Who I am, inside and out.

Scanning my experiences, the thoughts and the actions,

I find I must first be honest with myself,

If I am to truly face me.

I find this hard, as there are many things,

I wish I hadn't done or said;

But I also see how all the events,

Both those remembered fondly, and those wished forgotten,

All make up a facet of me.

Some I learned from, and grew from the experience,

Others were pure enjoyment, even if they weren't always wise.

Joys, fears, mistakes, and experiments;

Relationships, friendships, trials and errors;

I must face them with an open heart and mind,

And true acceptance of myself,

If I ever truly wish another to be able to do the same.

So I must over come the urge to simply forget,

Or to rationalize in my own mind

The errors of my past.

They are not me, but they help shape me;

Who I am and who I will be in the years to come,

So I must accept them, and move on.

Life Lost

A friend to me,

A flirt to many,

He was always a surprise.

On the dance floor,

Or bare foot on the beach;

We talked for hours

And kept the other from loneliness.

Now who will cheer him up,

And who will dance me around the room,

Now that he is gone?

I lost my friend on the day

He chose to take fate in his own hands.

The details of how

And more importantly of why

Are lost to me, and I may never know.

I simply know I lost my friend.

And I don't know what to think or feel.

He took his life

Without a word to anyone;

No cry of help for any to hear.

So many times we spent

Talking on for hours

Discussing all in life.

Not once did I suspect

I would ever hear news like this.

Before he left did he think of his friends?

Of those that would feel his absence the most?

The last time we spoke things were going well,

He was pleased with life and its positive direction:

He had a new place to live,

He was doing well at his new job,

And he had a new girl in his life

That brought a smile to his face.

These things, to me, sound like a life going well,

Yet the next thing I hear, he is forever gone.

Never once did I expect,

Never once did I see a sign,

Yet out of the blue, I lost a friend;

And I have yet to cry.

Upon hearing the news,

Denial hit first

Followed later by shock, when I was told twice more.

I wonder now, what I feel,

Because all that registers is loss.

I've lost some one that I called friend,

And I've lost my mind to thoughts of the past.

I'm reliving memories and going over conversations,

Both in memory of my missing friend,

And in search of a hint or sign that before I may have missed.

A clue that may have let me know

And perhaps let me help prevent

The events that recently occurred.

Part of me knows this thinking is crazy,

But I search the past anyways;

To process my thoughts, my memories, and his loss.

I have been writing of many things,

As I try to make sense

Of me, of him, of life, and death.

I Need You

I need your embrace today,

And your assurance that it will be okay.

I need your presence soon,

And your warmth to calm me as my mind unwinds.

I need your smile to make me smile,

And your eyes to assure me I'm loved.

I need you to hold me,

Until I'm no longer crying;

And I need you to love me,

Until I remember only joy.

The Personal Turmoil of Loss

Experiencing loss seems to cause

People to act in peculiar ways

That they are bound to question later.

Saying and doing things

They would usually not,

Like acting out, or closing down.

I've lost my temper many times

When usually it is held under check;

My patience, usually a mile thick

Has unexplainably warn thin,

And I find my self wanting to be alone,

Or immersed in a large crowd.

My emotions have gotten lost on a detour

And have yet to catch back up to me,

While my mind wanders through the past

Trying to find the answers to everything

No matter the subject or why.

In the mess of it all, I also find

That my body craves the touch of another,

The feel of a connection to this life and this world

I am left to wonder if any, none, or all of these things

Will provide any assistance to me

In the process of accepting this grief

And moving on past the turmoil it causes.

Slowly I try to address each step,

Finding that I fall short on them all.

What if no matter what I do

I cannot get past

This feeling of falling upside down?

How can I catch my balance,

If I can't find my feet,

And there is no floor?

A Toast

Stepping forward

And stepping up

I challenge my world

And raise my cup.

"To the past

That hasn't always gone so well,

To the future

That no one can tell,

And above all else

A toast to the now,

Built on our yesterdays,

And for our futures, provide the how."

I could sit and wait

For the future to arrive

But I won't reach my true destination

If I never truly try . . .

Lost

. . . .

I am not me, I am lost.

Me was sent for I, but never returned.

In their place, there lies a mask

What people see as me, but truth be told, . . .

I'm still lost.

I used the past as my anchor,

But the ropes were severed.

With nothing left to hold on to,

I drift away into the unknown of my future.

My only guide being me . . .

No wonder I feel so lost.

Time

Time . . . where have you go to

And where are you headed?

You always seem to change your pace,

But really you move at a constant rate.

The moment is now in the past,

And time moves too fast;

Making it impossible

To catch up with the past.

JDS

You came in, and turned my heart around,
Then you left, putting my heart up side down.
Why this is so, I may never know;
But life goes on, and I am on my own.

Tell me why the earth goes round the sun,
Why the sun rises in the east,
And why the sky is blue.
Then can you explain to me,
Why I can only think of you.

Gone

I spent all my tears crying that night
To ease my mind, I put my nose in a book.
When that method only failed,
I wrote it all down, and gave it one last look.
Before tucking it away . . . forever.

What I See

Not everyone loves you,

The way that I do;

They must not see what I see,

When I look at you.

Dusk

As the day comes to an end,

I sit and I watch now and then.

The day descends.

Night Time

Moonbeams scattered across the night sky;

Bringing wonderful pleasure, by and by.

I relax and sigh.

Betrayed

Once two good friends say hello,

Then you will see how low she can go;

She'll show you so.

The Future

The future can be your destiny,

Some of the time it's just not great to see.

So just let it be.

Frozen Moments

Looking back, I see it all

The haze of time puts me in a trance

But these pictures on my bed

Bring the past back in a glance.

This one took my breath away

As no amount of time can erase

The feelings rushing back to me,

At the sight of your face.

We call them moments, they hang on the wall

Kept frozen in time, the memories made to recall.

But it's the ones we hide, with so much to say

Thought of deep in the night, not in the day

It's only time, no longer lost, but found.

Each photo a memory, one by one, they fall to the ground.

One look is all it takes, and the past comes flooding back,

It's not forgotten, no, never forgotten.

One look, that's all it takes, and my pictures come alive.

Dancing through our evenings,

Lost in your eyes and loving your touch,

Those days are here all around me,

And yet just memories, that still mean so much.

Our days in the sun, and nights in your arms

Our smiles and laughs forever are cast

In pictures, like my feelings, I keep hidden,

For my love is forever captured, in our past.

We call them moments, they hang on the wall

Kept frozen in time, the memories made to recall.

But it's the ones we hide, with so much to say

Thought of deep in the night, not in the day

It's only time, no longer lost, but found.

Each photo a memory, one by one, they fall to the ground.

One look is all it takes, and the past comes flooding back,

It's not forgotten, no, never forgotten.

One look, that's all it takes, and my pictures come alive.

A picture holds a thousand words but this one holds just one,

That afternoon laying in your arms, laughing in the clover

Once brought such joy, but now all I feel is loss

Knowing that our time is gone, knowing that we are over.

It's only time, no longer lost, but found.

Each photo a memory, one by one, they fall to the ground.

One look is all it takes, and the past comes flooding back,

It's not forgotten, no, never forgotten.

One look, that's all it takes, and my pictures come alive.

We call them moments, they hang on the wall

Kept frozen in time, the memories made to recall.

So why do I still sit here, wishing you would call?

Knowing, always knowing

You will never call.

Heart Beat

My head on your chest, I hear your heart beat remind me of the peace I find in your arms

I want to take this second chance I have been given, to find happiness ever after with you

The loss in my past looms over me, as I try to move forward, out of the turmoil inside me

Don't rush in, that's been done before, first I need to know if what we feel is true

So take a walk with me, side by side we will stay.

When our paths are pulled apart, faith and trust in each other

Will keep our hearts safe and together.

Be with me, and ease my mind, and I will care for you for all of time.

My heart is not fragile, but it certainly is weary, afraid to go out on that ledge alone

Will you join me for the jump, no net to catch us, when we take that leap to the future

I cannot find the words to give you, in relation to my heart's attachment to you already

Though I fear the future is shaky, I trust in you, as I know your heart is sweet and pure

> So take a walk with me, side by side we will stay.
> When our paths are pulled apart, faith and trust in each other
> Will keep our hearts safe and together.
> Be with me, and ease my mind, and I will care for you for all of time.

Though I fear the future is shaky, I trust in you, and I think we can make it together
I do not give my heart easily, but it seems you have it anyway, and I am okay
So be careful my love, feel it beat in your chest,
And always remember, that together I'm sure, we can handle the rest.

Every Day is New

The sun rises on possibilities each day,

Don't let it set on a list of unfulfilled wishes;

You don't have to climb Everest in order to seize the day,

Just know the day is a miracle, one that will never be repeated.

Mundane events blur our days, one into another;

To make each day a memory that lasts,

You must do something extraordinary yet simple.

Take a walk and think, take a drive and sing,

Each with no hurry nor destination;

Pick up a paint brush, or write something sweet,

Try something new to you, or seldom done.

Forget your age, and go out to play,

Parks are made for everyone;

Ignore all else and dance in the street

With only the moon and an owl keeping you company.

There is nothing stopping you from truly relaxing

Or simply letting go.

Each day is what we make of it, so I say it is time to go.

Time to go and seize each moment, we only hold ourselves back.

Give yourself permission to live a little more each day

And soon nothing will ever be tedious again.

Soon we will find even the once mundane

Has turned itself into a secret joy to share

And you will realize you are more than relaxed

With each new breath of fresh morning air.

Enjoy the Earth: it's weather and sky,

It's land and waters, and every creature that can be a surprise;

Relax in the spring time sun, and smile into the summer storm,

Every second only happens once,

Live it well, and know the truth:

Each day is a miracle, filled with possibilities, just for you.

So I ask you this: In this moment, what do you really want to do?

About the Author

. . . .

Dominique is a strong and remarkable person and mother who has been through a lot in the last few years. Her determination and her love for her son, Nathanial, who is now four years old, keeps her going day to day. No matter what they face in their lives, her love for her son is the strongest constant in her life. While still in Mississippi, Dominique looks forward to the day she can resume her travels of the world, and show her son the treasures that her parents spent their lives showing her.